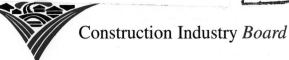

Construction Industry *Board*

Code of practice for the selection of subcontractors

April 1997

Thomas Telford

Published for the Construction Industry Board by Thomas Telford Publishing, Thomas Telford Services Ltd, 1 Heron Quay, London E14 4JD

First published 1997

Distributors for Thomas Telford books are
USA: American Society of Civil Engineers, Publications Sales Department, 345 East 47th Street, New York, NY 10017-2398
Japan: Maruzen Co. Ltd, Book Department, 3–10 Nihonbashi 2-chome, Chuo-ku, Tokyo 103
Australia: DA Books and Journals, 648 Whitehorse Road, Mitcham 3132, Victoria

A catalogue record for this book is available from the British Library

ISBN: 0 7277 2543 2

© Construction Industry Board Ltd, 1997

Typeset by Gray Publishing, Tunbridge Wells, Kent
Printed in Great Britain by Spottiswoode Ballantyne Printers Ltd, Colchester, Essex

Contents

Glossary

The Key Players

Client
The customer for construction.

Consultant
An individual or organisation providing design, cost, management or other advisory services.

Contractor
Any individual or organisation that contracts to undertake or manage construction work. For ease of reading the term is used in this code to denote the main contractor, who is contracted by the client to construct the works, and who in turn will usually contract with subcontractors.

Designer
An architect, engineer, specialist consultant or contractor responsible for the design of part or all of a project.

Lead contractor
The organisation that contracts with the client to construct (and sometimes design) the project. The lead contractor will usually engage subcontractors to construct (and sometimes design) specific parts of the project.

Main contractor
The lead contractor in 'design and build' and in 'traditional', designer-led procurement.

Preferred tenderer
A tenderer selected to proceed towards a contract, subject to discussion. This might include negotiation of the scope or the pricing of the contract, or collaboration in the development of the final design (as in two stage tendering).

Specialist contractor
An individual or organisation which specialises in the construction (and frequently design) of a particular part of a project, and which may be employed either as a subcontractor or directly by the client.

Subcontractor
An individual or organisation employed by the lead contractor to construct (and sometimes design) part of a project.

Sub-subcontractor
An individual or organisation employed by a subcontractor to construct (and sometimes design) part of a project.

Technical Terms

Approved list
A list of contractors who have qualified to carry out construction work for a client. The list is normally categorised according to the type and value that the contractor is competent to undertake.

Competitive tendering
The process of inviting tenders from more than one tenderer to undertake work or provide services; preparation of tenders by the tenderers; and their receipt by the client.

Compliant tender
A tender that complies in every respect with the requirements set out in the tender enquiry documents.

Construction
The process of constructing a building or civil engineering project, including new structures, maintenance, repair and refurbishment.

Construction project
A series of activities to define, design, construct and put to use of construction work.

Partnering
A relationship between parties to a project in which they work openly and jointly to achieve common objectives, with defined performance targets. Partnering may be entered into for a single project or a series of projects.

Procurement system
A method of obtaining and organising the external resources needed to complete a project.

Qualification
The process of assessing potential contractors as suitable and competent to undertake certain types and values of construction work against general, rather than project-specific, criteria.

Risk management
A systematic procedure to identify, assess, control and manage risk on a project in order to minimise potential damage or loss.

Selection
The whole process of identifying the best tenderer from the available field, through qualification, compiling the tender list, tendering and assessment. At some points in this code the term is restricted by its context to refer only to the final stages of tendering and identification of the best tenderer.

Single round tendering
A process in which tenderers are asked to submit competitive tenders at one point only. It may be preceded by comparative assessments in the course of compiling the tender list (as in qualification), and may be followed by negotiation prior to agreement of the contract (as in two stage tendering).

Single stage tendering
A tendering process intended to lead directly to the award of a contract to the successful tenderer for the works described in the tender enquiry documents.

Standard forms of contract
Printed forms of contract published by industry organisations and intended for general use in defining the obligations of the parties to a contract to carry out construction work. Different forms are intended for different types of project. Suites of contracts are becoming available that cover the obligations between all parties in a construction project (including client, lead contractor, subcontractors, consultants and others).

Tender list
A limited number of potential tenderers who are invited to submit tenders. Methods of compiling the list vary according to the circumstances of the client and the project, and might be preceded by open advertising and/or drawing from an approved list.

Two stage tendering
A tendering process in which the first stage is to select a preferred tenderer before the design is fully developed, on the basis of indicative pricing documents. In the second stage the preferred tenderer collaborates with the designers to complete the design and agrees firm prices as the basis of the contract for construction.

1 Introduction

This code of practice is one of a set of documents from the CIB aimed at improving the quality, effectiveness and efficiency of the construction industry. It should be used in conjunction with the other documents in the series.[1-4] The good practice recommended should be observed in commercial relationships throughout the contractual chain and throughout the duration of a construction project.

Subcontractors can be selected by competitive tendering, by negotiation or as a result of partnering or a joint venture arrangement. Competitive tendering is complex and requires everyone involved to follow a common set of procedures; inevitably it occupies the bulk of this code. In competitive tendering for small or simple works all the steps described are required but many may take place informally, and these are indicated by dotted lines in the diagrams which accompany each section of the code. Negotiation, partnering or joint ventures should all be carried out in the same spirit of good practice although specific procedures will vary.

For competitive tendering to be effective in providing good value for money it must be seen to be fair and the processes by which decisions are reached must be as open as possible. This applies to all forms of subcontractor selection.

Key principles of good practice in selecting subcontractors are that:

- clear procedures that ensure fair and transparent competition in a single round of tendering consisting of one or more stages should be followed
- the tendering process should ensure receipt of compliant, competitive tenders
- tender lists should be compiled systematically from a number of qualified candidates
- tender lists should be as short as possible
- conditions for all tenderers should be the same
- confidentiality should be respected by all parties
- sufficient time and information should be provided to allow the preparation of tenders appropriate to the type of works
- tenders should be assessed and accepted having regard to quality as well as price
- practices that avoid or discourage collusion should be followed
- tender prices should not change on an unaltered scope of works
- proposed contracts should be compatible and consistent with the main contract
- suites of contracts and standard unamended contract forms from recognised bodies should be used where they are available
- there should be a commitment to team work from all parties.

All construction projects involve risk in a variety of areas. Risk management, the appropriate assessment and apportionment of these risks, is essential to the success of any project.

[1] *Briefing the team.* Thomas Telford, 1997

[2] *Constructing success: code of practice for clients of the construction industry.* Thomas Telford, 1997

[3] *Code of practice for the selection of main contractors.* Thomas Telford, 1997

[4] *Selecting consultants for the team.* Thomas Telford, 1996

The code deals specifically with the selection of subcontractors by main contractors and the selection of sub-subcontractors by subcontractors, with particular emphasis on competitive tendering. Selection forms only part of the whole process of construction; the overall success of projects depends on other parts of the process being carried out in the same co-operative spirit. The code stresses the need for clarity and certainty at all times, whichever procurement system is chosen.

Compliance with this code will result in practices such as multiple round tendering, bid peddling or 'Dutch auctioning' being rendered unacceptable.

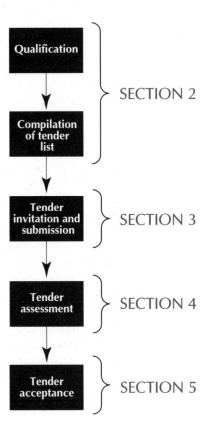

Figure 1. The selection process

Background, objectives and scope

1.1 A code of practice for the selection of subcontractors was recommended by Sir Michael Latham in his 1994 report *Constructing the Team*.[5] His recommendations have been carried forward by the Construction Industry Board (CIB) and it is the CIB which has commissioned and endorsed this code.

1.2 The objective of the code is to improve the efficiency of the construction industry through good practice, to eliminate duplication and waste and to increase the satisfaction of both clients and the industry with the process and the outcome of construction. All these factors imply a need for changes in the way the industry performs.

1.3 The code sets out the principles of how main contractors and subcontractors, and subcontractors and sub-subcontractors, should deal with each other throughout the selection process. A subcontractor undertakes all or part of the works, by way of contract, for a main contractor; a sub-subcontractor carries out work, by way of contract, for a subcontractor. For the sake of clarity this code refers only to contractors (the employing party) and subcontractors (the employed party) throughout the contractual chain. It specifically addresses the selection of domestic subcontractors whose selection is solely the responsibility of the contractor.

1.4 The code seeks to foster an environment where tenderers will submit timely, competitive, compliant tenders at the outset and, in return, contractors will deal fairly and openly with tenderers. A compliant tender is one that is in accordance with the tender enquiry documents in all respects. Where the option is permitted by the contractor, compliant tenders may be accompanied by tenders based on alternative approaches. Compliance with the code will render practices such as multiple rounds of tendering or 'Dutch auctioning' unacceptable.

1.5 The code applies to the selection of subcontractors for different types of works, ranging from those involving labour only to those requiring a substantial specialist design input. It is not directed at procurement systems where anyone other than a main contractor or subcontractor carries out the selection process, or where other contractual relationships are to be implemented (e.g. the selection of nominated subcontractors, trade contractors under management-type contracting arrangements or designers where they are employed as subcontractors), but the key principles still apply.

1.6 The principles of good practice embodied in the code are relevant and should be applied to every contract regardless of size, although without creating unnecessary administration. The code applies to the selection of subcontractors for works above £10,000 in value (excluding VAT). The total value of subcontracts placed for a trade or package of work should not be split into smaller lots in order to avoid the application of this code.

1.7 Contractors need subcontractors of sufficient calibre and with appropriate resources to execute the necessary works at a price and quality that will enable contractors to be competitive in their overall tender to the client. Any selection and tender process requires fair dealing between parties as a basis for successful teamwork and the avoidance of disputes.

1.8 In many cases contractors invite tenders from subcontractors at a stage when they themselves are not yet – and may never be – appointed to undertake the work. In these circumstances the time available for tendering, and the

[5]Sir Michael Latham. HMSO, 1994.

information that can be provided to tenderers, is often not in the direct control of the contractor. All the stages in the subcontract tendering process described in this code depend on the constraints to which the contractor seeking tenders is subject. If a contractor is given insufficient time or information by a client for the preparation of tenders, the effectiveness of the subcontractor selection process will suffer.

1.9 Competitive tenders should only be invited if there is a genuine intention to select a subcontractor on that basis. A contractor, while not bound to accept the lowest or any tender, should have the clear intention of accepting one of them. When firm tenders have been obtained, a contractor should not seek new tenders after being appointed.

1.10 When contractors request indicative prices, they should make it clear that they are not seeking a firm tender price on which selection will be based but requesting help in putting together a proposal for their own client, and that no guarantee of future work is being offered. If payment for this service is considered appropriate, an agreement to that effect should be made at the outset.

1.11 Competitive tendering is only one of a variety of approaches to selecting a sub-contractor. A contractor may wish to use an organisation with which it has a partnering arrangement, or to negotiate a contract; a joint venture may also be considered. Nonetheless, the principles of this code are relevant to all processes and should be followed whenever a contractor selects a subcontractor.

1.12 Single stage tendering is generally the most appropriate form of competitive tendering, but two-stage tendering may be suitable for large, complex schemes where early involvement of the contracting team is required prior to the completion of the full design. Where the early involvement of a specialist contractor is required for design services or other specialist practical advice, this is best provided for by direct agreement between those parties based on a separate selection process.

1.13 With two-stage tendering the first stage of selection is based on pricing documents related to preliminary design information. These provide the level of prices on which to base a final price once the design has been completed. Selection for the second stage does not imply that a contract for the works has been entered into.

1.14 Competitive tendering may be impossible or inappropriate, for example when only one organisation has the expertise or resources required or when works or services are required urgently and there is not enough time to undertake the competitive process properly.

1.15 In the interests of efficiency and overall cost reduction, appropriate use should be made of new technologies as they develop. For example, consideration should be given to supplying documents or drawings electronically to reduce bulky sets of tendering papers and to enable copies to be made easily.

1.16 Throughout the selection process, tender information provided by all parties must be treated as confidential by everyone concerned.

1.17 Design by potential subcontractors may be a critical element in the construction process. Where such specialist design is required, it is desirable that these specialists are involved at the earliest possible stage. Adequate time for tender and design preparation is essential and those designing must be provided with clear briefing.

1.18 Copyright of any design prepared by tenderers will automatically vest in them. It will not transfer even if they have been paid for the design unless such transfer has been expressly agreed.

2

Qualification and the compilation of the tender list

Recognition of the importance of the quality as well as the price of a product or service is a prime requirement in the selection of tenderers. Assessing potential subcontractors for their general skills and performance is an important part of any selection process. For competitive tendering the aim should be to identify a minimum number of comparable, competent, suitable organisations willing and able to tender from whom compliant tenders will be received, so that good value for money can be achieved while containing the costs of the tendering process.

All tenderers should be informed when the selection process includes an in-house tenderer; such a tenderer should not benefit from any unfair advantage. Contractors using approaches other than competitive tendering, such as negotiation, partnering or a joint venture, should be equally committed to selecting an appropriate, qualified subcontractor able to contribute to best value for money.

The criteria to be used in assessing tenders should be notified during the selection process and stated in the tender enquiry documents.

Good practice on the part of a client includes the provision of adequate time for each step detailed in this code. Clients should appreciate the close relationship between the time allowed for preparation of tenders and their subsequent quality. Where a contractor has insufficient time to follow the procedures set out in the code, the final quality of the project is likely to suffer. Where a project is simple and works or services are straightforward, some of the steps shown in Fig. 2 may take place informally.

Key principles of good practice that apply to qualification and to the compilation of the tender list are that:

- clear procedures that ensure fair and transparent competition in a single round of tendering consisting of one or more stages should be followed
- the tendering process should ensure the receipt of compliant, competitive tenders
- tender lists should be compiled systematically from a number of qualified candidates
- tender lists should be as short as possible
- conditions for all potential tenderers should be the same
- sufficient time and information should be provided to allow the preparation of tenders appropriate to the type of works.

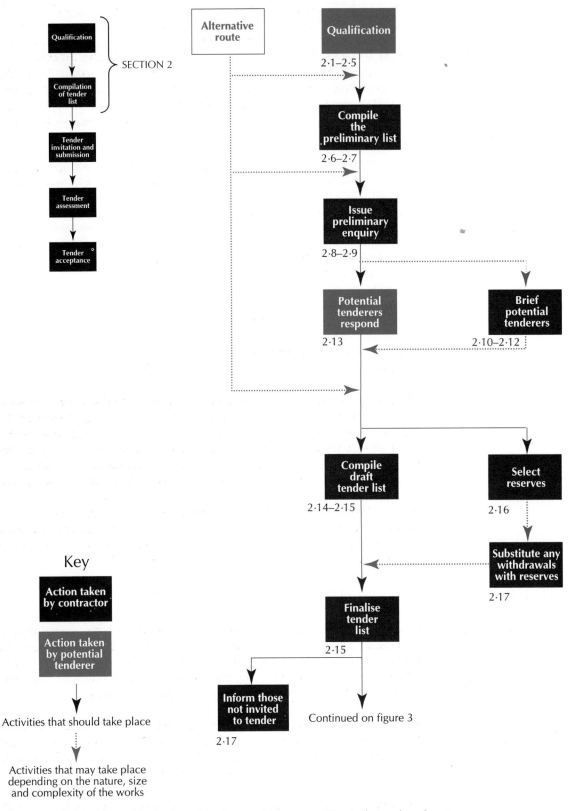

Figure 2. Qualification and selection of tenderers where competition is the preferred route

Qualification

2.1 Qualification is the process of assessing potential subcontractors for their general skills and competence, to establish their suitability to undertake given types of construction work within predetermined ranges of values. It is carried out against general, rather than project-specific, criteria and can be used to compile an approved list of those who might be called upon to tender for the type(s) of work for which they are qualified. It is intended to ensure that all those who are invited to tender are capable of performing to the required standard, and that the tender lists for competitive tendering comprise a comparable group of tenderers of appropriate standing and with established skill, integrity, responsibility and competence.

2.2 Potential tenderers should be qualified on the basis of their own skills and, where applicable, their ability to select suitably qualified subcontractors.

2.3 Criteria for qualification should include:

- quality of work
- performance record
- overall competence
- health and safety record
- financial stability
- appropriate insurance cover
- size and resources
- technical and organisational ability
- ability to innovate.

2.4 The process of qualification is important whether candidates are to be invited to tender competitively or are appointed on any other basis, e.g. negotiation. Contractors who neither maintain nor have access to an appropriate approved list will need to follow a formal and systematic qualification process as a preliminary to compiling the tender list. In particular they should take steps to ensure that potential tenderers meet the desired thresholds in the criteria set out in 2.3.

2.5 Approved lists should be reviewed regularly, and those organisations which are added or removed should be formally notified. Where formal registration schemes exist, such as trade association lists, these may provide a suitable basis for an approved list.

Compiling the tender list

2.6 A preliminary list should be selected from an appropriate pool of qualified candidates. For more complex subcontracts there may be several stages to be carried out in establishing this list. Past performance may not always provide all the necessary information; some briefing or discussion may be required to test the suitability of proposed tenderers for particular works.

2.7 The cost of preparing tenders is a significant element in the cost of construction. Open competition, with no limit on the number of tenderers invited, is expensive and time-consuming for all. Tender lists should, therefore, be short so that only a limited number of tenderers incur preparation costs.

2.8 Potential tenderers from the preliminary list should be asked if they are willing to tender. The purpose of this enquiry is to seek information from qualified tenderers about their current and anticipated available capacity, what team could be available, and their grasp of, and enthusiasm for, the proposed works.

11

2.9   Potential tenderers require sufficient information to enable them to decide if they wish to tender. They should be assured that where formal tenders are invited these will be assessed in accordance with this code. The information given at this stage should include, when known:

- job name and location
- nature, scope and approximate value of the subcontract works including reference to the extent of any design work required
- likely dates and duration of both the tendering process and the subcontract works
- number of tenderers invited to submit a formal tender
- whether the contractor is already appointed or is involved in a tendering process
- main contract tender date
- approximate value and period of the main contract
- whether, and how, any costs may be shared
- whether the tender will be based on bills of quantities or other pricing documents or on specification and drawings
- selection procedure and selection criteria
- main and subcontract conditions
- names of the client and the relevant consultants.

2.10   Briefing, the exchange of relevant information, may be helpful, so that when tender enquiry documents are issued they are capable of leading to compliant tenders. Contractors should ensure that their requirements are fully explained, that there is mutual understanding of the proposed works and that, where necessary, an opportunity is provided to discuss possible methods. Where contractors and potential subcontractors are known to each other and have worked together recently on comparable projects, there will be less need for such discussions.

2.11   Briefing sessions may be appropriate where they can provide additional clarity and information for either party and thereby increase the likelihood of compliant tenders. This is especially relevant where a project is large or complex, or where a specialist subcontractor will have substantial design input. If the parties involved are not familiar with each other, such sessions can also help to establish more clearly whether they would be suitable and compatible team members. In some cases it can be beneficial to visit a potential tenderer's place of business or site operations.

2.12   Briefing sessions should be carefully planned in order to gain the maximum benefit. They should be conducted with a standard agenda to ensure consistent treatment. They should involve individuals with relevant responsibility for the project, for example those with design or co-ordination expertise if this is important.

2.13   When potential tenderers have been identified for a draft tender list they should be asked for confirmation of their willingness to tender. If a potential tenderer cannot tender despite having indicated willingness to do so, the contractor should be notified before the issue of full tender enquiry documents.

2.14   The appropriate length of tender lists varies according to the types of works or services envisaged. Lists should be as short as possible, consistent with the objective of receiving a sufficient number of compliant tenders. They should generally be shorter where the requirements are more complex and, therefore, the tendering process more costly. A guide to the number of invitations to issue and compliant tenders required for effective competition is given in the table below.

Subcontract type	Maximum number of invitations to issue	Minimum number of compliant tenders required
Design only	4	3
Construct only (including minor design/proprietary supply)	6	4
Design and construct	3	2

These numbers are not always appropriate. For example, it may not be possible to find the number of qualified organisations shown; or in the 'construct only' category, shorter lists may be appropriate for smaller or very large contracts.

2.15   It should not be necessary to invite more than six tenders for each contract. If the minimum number of compliant tenders is received the contractor should not seek more.

2.16   A list of reserve tenderers should be identified. For a tender list of up to three, one reserve is adequate, for a longer list, two are sufficient. Reserves should be informed that they have been selected as reserves and that they will not be asked to tender unless any of those on the tender list drop out.

2.17   Reserves may also be needed if a tenderer wishes to withdraw during the process. Reserves must have sufficient time to complete the tendering process. Those who have expressed willingness, but are not included in the tender list, should be informed promptly.

2.18   If tender enquiry documents are not dispatched within three months of the date of a potential tenderer's confirmation of willingness to tender, those on the list should be asked to reconfirm their willingness to tender.

3 Tender invitation and submission

Competitive tendering is directed at obtaining compliant tenders from suitable tenderers by means of a single round of tendering. This objective requires the best available information to be prepared and issued under identical conditions to all organisations tendering for the work.

The procedures for submission of tenders and the criteria for assessment should be clear to all concerned, and should be applied equally to all tenderers.

To ensure that tenderers submit their best tenders, practices such as multiple rounds of tendering should be eliminated. Commitment is also needed from tenderers to submit a well considered and compliant tender.

Key principles of good practice that apply to tender invitation and submission are that:

- conditions for all tenderers should be the same
- confidentiality should be respected by all parties
- sufficient time and information should be provided to allow the preparation of tenders appropriate to the type of works
- practices that avoid or discourage collusion should be followed
- proposed contracts should be compatible and consistent with the main contract
- suites of contracts and standard unamended contract forms from recognised bodies should be used where they are available.

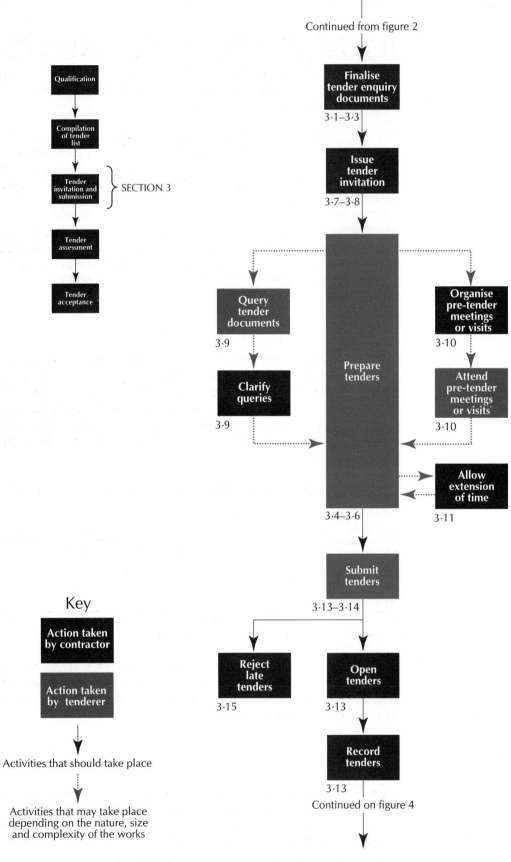

Figure 3. Tender invitation and submission

Tender enquiry documents

3.1 Tender enquiry documents should include at least the information detailed in Annex 1. The extent to which any information is approximate should be made clear. The documents should also state clearly what level of detail is required in the tender submission and whether the tenderer should provide priced schedules as well as a lump sum price.

3.2 The better the quality of information provided by the contractor and the more reasonable the time allowed for preparation of tenders, the greater the likelihood that compliant tenders will be received. If there is a need for additional time or information, which is unavailable to the contractor, this should be brought to the attention of the client.

3.3 Standard forms of tender can assist in ensuring comparable information from tenderers and, where possible, such forms should be used. Whichever form of tender is used, tender enquiry documents must be unambiguous, consistent and as complete as possible. This facilitates compliant tenders.

Time for tender preparation

3.4 The time required for tendering will vary according to the precise nature of the project. More time, however, may be required to prepare tenders where a project is large or complex, where specialist design input is needed, or where products and materials have to be sourced from unfamiliar or distant suppliers or sub-subcontractors. When a contractor has not yet been engaged for the works, the time available for subcontract tender preparation will depend on the contractor's own tendering process.

3.5 Suitable periods to allow for tendering for most projects are given in the table below.

Subcontract type	Minimum tender time: weeks
Design only	3
Construct only (including minor design/proprietary supply)	6
Design and construct	10

Shorter periods can be appropriate for small or less complex projects. A longer period may be required if a bank or industry holiday falls within the period.

3.6 Contractors need time before and after the subcontract tender period to carry out their part of the process. Clients and their advisers should take account of this by incorporating the above times within the time allowed to contractors for the preparation of their own tenders.

The tender invitation

3.7 The invitation to tender should be issued on the same day to all tenderers. The documents should state whether alternative tenders are acceptable. Such alternative tenders may be submitted in conjunction with, but never instead of, compliant ones. Tenderers should acknowledge receipt of the documents and confirm their willingness to submit a compliant tender.

3.8 The documents should state whether any tenderers are to be interviewed and, if so, for what purpose and at what stage. Such interviews must not be used as a form of second round tendering.

3.9 If a tenderer finds that any of the tender enquiry documents require clarification the contractor must be informed as soon as possible and not later than seven days before the date for submission of tenders. All queries from tenderers concerning ambiguity or errors in the documents, or the need for supplementary information, should be in writing, as should all responses which must be circulated to all tenderers. If the contractor decides to amend the documents, all tenderers must be informed and, if possible and necessary, the time for the submission of tenders extended. Amendments should be avoided if possible and should only be issued if they could materially affect tenders. The documents should include a deadline after which requests for additional information will not be considered.

3.10 If meetings or site visits are necessary, contractors should make the arrangements in good time.

3.11 If adequate time has been allowed for preparation of tenders there should be no need for an extension of time. If several tenderers ask for extensions, however, this may indicate that more time is needed in order to produce fully considered tenders. In this case the contractor should consider requesting an extension to their own tender period if this would be affected. Where any extension of time is granted it should be notified formally to all tenderers. Extension to the contractor's tender period should also be advised to tenderers even if no extension for them is required or granted.

Tender submission and opening

3.12 Confidentiality should be respected by all parties. For example any use of 'cover prices' is a breach of confidentiality. Tender prices should not be disclosed before contract award.

3.13 Tenders should be submitted in sealed packages and clearly labelled as tenders for the works. It should not be possible to identify tenderers' names from the packages. Tenders should be kept in a secure place and not opened before the date and time stated for receipt. When they are opened, forms of tender should be signed and prices should be listed against the names of the tenderers. This list should be signed by the person opening the tenders. Where possible, a second person should also be present and sign the forms of tender and the list.

3.14 Bills of quantities should only be required to be completed if they were supplied with the documents and it was stated that they should be part of the submission.

Late tenders

3.15 A date and time must be specified as the deadline for return of tenders and tenders received after that time should not be accepted.

4 Tender assessment

The assessment of tenders should have regard to both quality and price. The principles of balancing quality and price are relevant to the selection of sub-contractors; for further guidance see the CIB document *Selecting consultants for the team: balancing quality and price.*[6]

The process outlined in section 3 aims to achieve a suitable number of compliant tenders from which to select an organisation to carry out the works. On the assumption that this has been achieved, and in order to be fair, only compliant tenders and alternative approaches, where specifically permitted by the tender invitation, should be considered. The procedure for assessing tenders must support this approach.

Key principles of good practice that apply to tender assessment are that:

- conditions for all tenderers should be the same
- confidentiality should be respected by all parties
- tender assessment should have regard to quality as well as price
- practices that avoid or discourage collusion should be followed
- tender prices should not change on an unaltered scope of works.

[6] *Selecting consultants for the team.* Thomas Telford, 1996

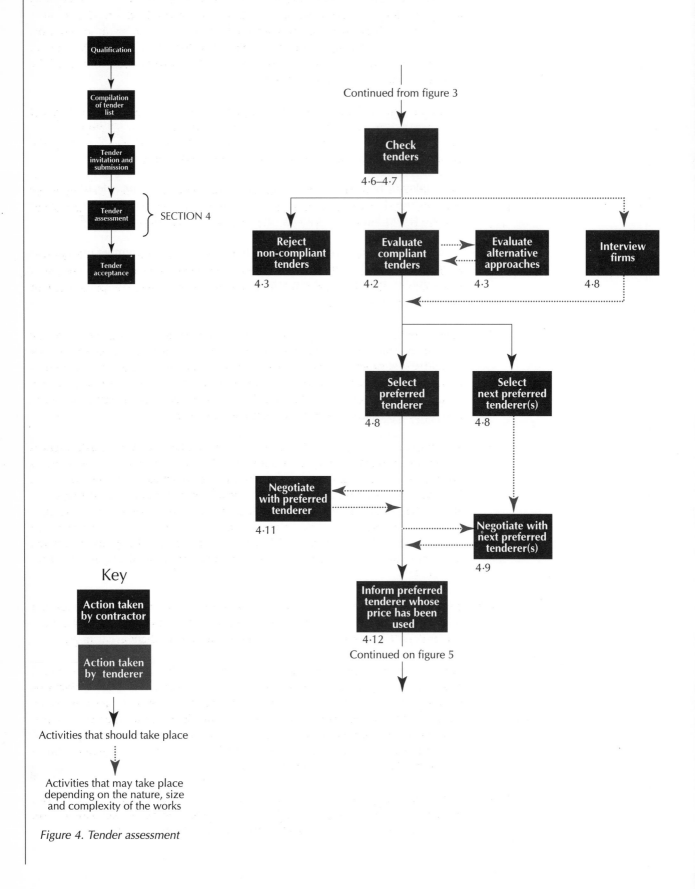

Figure 4. Tender assessment

Tender assessment

4.1   Tender assessment criteria, including the relative importance placed on quality and price, should have been advised to the tenderers in the tender enquiry documents. Where weighting of quality and price is to be applied, for example to take account of design input or specific expertise, the basis for this should be decided in advance and used consistently. A record should be kept of the scores awarded during the assessment.

4.2   Tenderers cannot be assessed on an equal basis unless tenders are submitted strictly in accordance with the tender enquiry documents in all respects – i.e. unless they are compliant. Compliant tenders should be assessed using the criteria already established in the tender enquiry documents.

4.3   Non-compliant tenders suggesting alternative approaches will only be considered when they accompany a compliant tender and are permitted. Any non-compliant tenders not accompanying a compliant tender should be rejected.

4.4   If insufficient compliant tenders are received the contractor may seek tenders from the reserve list. Alternatively, the contractor may ask tenderers whose non-compliant tenders have been rejected to make their tenders compliant without amendment of their price.

4.5   Unsolicited tenders are frequently submitted during the selection and tendering process, or after an order has been placed, by those tendering for the same work to another contractor. This practice is unacceptable under this code. It undermines the willingness of tenderers to put forward their best price in their initial tender. Subcontractors should not submit unsolicited tenders and contractors should make it clear that they will not consider them.

4.6   The arithmetic in compliant tenders should be checked. Where arithmetical errors are found these should be notified to the tenderer. In the tender enquiry documents the predominance of overall price or a schedule of rates will have been established. Where the overall price is the predominant factor the tenderer should be asked to stand by or withdraw the tender. Where rates are predominant, the contractor may request an amended tender price to accord with the rates given by the tenderer. Where there are errors of any other sort the contractor should consider carefully the effect of these if the tender were accepted.

4.7   Tenders should be compared with any pre-tender estimates and any serious and consistent discrepancy should be examined. Where there are obvious non-contenders it is possible to eliminate these and inform them accordingly.

4.8   Subcontractors should be selected on the basis of the assessment criteria set down. It may, however, be necessary to interview tenderers in order to clarify or amplify their submissions and select a preferred tenderer and a next preferred tenderer. Any interviews must be carefully controlled, in the same way as pre-tender briefing (*see paragraphs 2.10–2.12*) in order to avoid the suggestion or occurrence of supplementary rounds of tendering. Any matters agreed at interview should be recorded in writing.

4.9   Only where the preferred tenderer withdraws or post-tender negotiations break down is it necessary to approach the next preferred tenderer. If negotiations have taken place (*see paragraph 4.11*) then these may have to be repeated.

4.10   Wherever possible, tender prices on an unaltered scope of works should not change.

4.11   Changes to tender prices may be appropriate in exceptional circumstances, e.g. if the programme or scope of works alters in respect of specification, quantities or programme, or if more complete information becomes available. Changes may also be appropriate in following up an alternative tender from the preferred tenderer. Negotiations must be carefully planned and managed to retain confidence and trust and should avoid any disadvantage to other tenderers. They should only be undertaken under controlled conditions to avoid practices such as second round tendering.

4.12   Where a firm decision has been made to use a preferred subcontractor's tender in a contractor's tender submission to the client, the selected subcontractor should be notified. Unless requested by the client not to do so, the identity of the subcontractor whose price has been incorporated in the tender should be notified to the client.

4.13   If a tender has not been accepted by the contractor within the stated period of validity, preferred tenderers should be asked if they wish to allow the acceptance period to be extended without amendment, or withdraw, or submit a tender which takes account of any changes in prices to the tenderer.

5

Tender acceptance

Subcontract tendering takes place in different contexts. For example, the contractor may be using a tenderer's price to prepare a tender for a client. In this context it is unlikely that the contractor will wish to create a binding contract until their tender is formally accepted by the client. Alternatively, the contractor may already have been awarded a contract by the client. In this case the contractor may wish to accept the subcontractor's tender and thereby create a binding contract.

Key principles of good practice that apply to tender acceptance are that:

- tenders should be accepted having regard to quality as well as price
- proposed contracts should be compatible and consistent with the main contract
- suites of contracts and standard unamended contract forms from recognised bodies should be used where they are available.

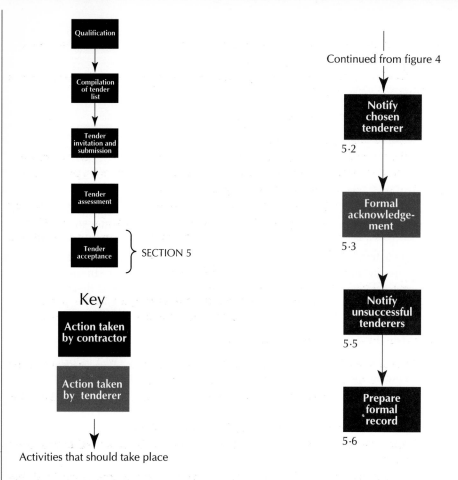

Figure 5. Tender acceptance

Tender acceptance

5.1 Where a contractor has incorporated an agreed tender price from a preferred tenderer in a main (or sub-) contract tender, and this is accepted, the contractor should accept that subcontract tender after the main (or sub-) contract award.

5.2 Formal notification should be sent to the preferred tenderer as soon as it has been decided to accept the tender.

5.3 When a tender is accepted by the contractor, a binding contract exists. The successful tenderer should issue an acknowledgement.

5.4 Following acknowledgement, a list of compliant tender prices and tenderers should be available to tenderers on request. The names of the tenderers should not be matched to the prices.

5.5 All unsuccessful tenderers should be informed if this has not already been done. Arrangements should be made with unsuccessful tenderers to destroy or return their tender documents. A debriefing document or session for unsuccessful tenderers can be valuable.

5.6 A formal record of the selection of the preferred tenderer should be prepared.

Annex 1   Tender enquiry documents

Invitations to tender should include the following documents and information:

1. A full list of the tender enquiry documents so that the tenderer can check that they are complete.

2. Instructions to tenderers, to include:

   * where and by when to submit the tender
   * the type of tender required, e.g. lump sum, priced bills, schedule of rates (and, if more than one of these is required, which will take precedence)
   * how the tender should be packaged and identified
   * how any errors or inconsistencies by the contractor in the tender enquiry documents, discovered after they have been issued, will be dealt with
   * whether alternative proposals are acceptable in conjunction with a compliant tender
   * the period of validity required for the tender
   * the target date for tender acceptance
   * details of arrangements for visiting the site during the tender period
   * whether the contractor is bound to accept the lowest or any tender.

3. Information for tenderers, to include:

   * the name of the person to provide the single point of contact within the contractor's organisation for all communication
   * whether the contractor is already appointed or, if not, target dates for tender acceptance
   * latest information available about the scope of work
   * approximate dates for commencement and completion of subcontract works
   * an opportunity for the tenderer to provide a programme of works if this has not been supplied
   * any requirement to have a preferred tenderer approved
   * the contract conditions to be used
   * if amendments to the standard form or suite of forms are proposed, they should be specifically identified
   * dispute resolution procedures, if not incorporated in the contract
   * whether price fluctuations will apply and, if so, how
   * payment terms, including information about retentions, retention bonds, advance payments for materials, security of payment and protection against non-payment
   * any requirements for bonds, guarantees, insurances etc.
   * the terms and conditions of supply of any pre-ordered equipment and materials
   * site attendance facilities to be provided to, or by, the subcontractor
   * tender assessment criteria
   * how any tenderer's errors will be handled
   * how tender results will be communicated.

4. Standards and specifications

5. Schedules and drawings, including any pricing schedules required by the form of contract (e.g. bills of quantities)

6. The health and safety plan, a requirement of the *Construction (Design and Management) Regulations 1994*, including the identity of the planning supervisor, if known.

7. Form of tender

Annex 2   Process of selection of subcontractors

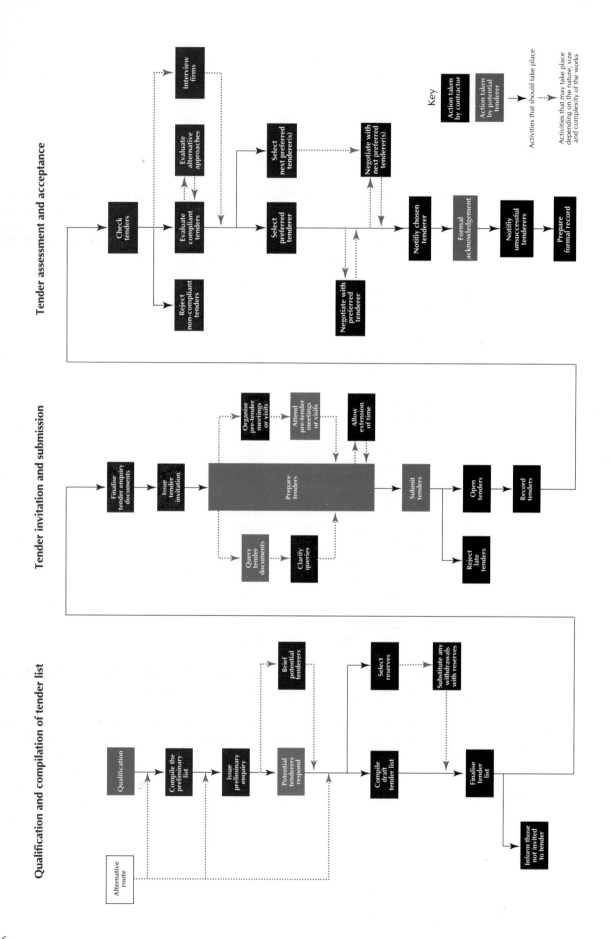

Tender assessment and acceptance

Check tenders → Evaluate compliant tenders → Select preferred tenderer → Notify chosen tenderer → Formal acknowledgement → Notify unsuccessful tenderers → Prepare formal record

Interview firms

Evaluate alternative approaches

Select next preferred tenderer(s) → Negotiate with next preferred tenderer(s)

Reject non-compliant tenders

Negotiate with preferred tenderer

Key

Action taken by contractor

Action taken by potential tenderer

→ Activities that should take place

⋯⋯▸ Activities that may take place depending on the nature, size and complexity of the works

Tender invitation and submission

Finalise tender enquiry documents → Issue tender invitation → Prepare tenders → Submit tenders → Open tenders → Record tenders

Organise pre-tender meetings or visits

Attend pre-tender meetings or visits

Allow extension of time

Query tender documents → Clarify queries

Reject late tenders

Qualification and compilation of tender list

Qualification → Compile the preliminary list → Issue preliminary enquiry → Potential tenderers respond → Compile draft tender list → Finalise tender list

Brief potential tenderers

Select reserves → Substitute any withdrawals with reserves

Inform those not invited to tender

Alternative route

26

Acknowledgements

This report is an output of Working Group 3 of the Construction Industry Board, one of twelve such teams established to implement specific recommendations from Sir Michael Latham's 1994 report *Constructing the Team*. Most members of WG3 were nominated by the umbrella bodies which now constitute the Construction Industry Board, and they were as follows:

Chairman:

Chris Sneath	CLG

Secretaries:

Rosemary Beales	CIEC
Marion Rich	CLG

Members:

John Deal	CIC
David Sherwood	CIC
Martin Wade	CIC
David Avery	CIEC
Ivan Dickason	CIEC
George May	CIEC
Ian Ross	CIEC
David Berryman	CLG
Gerrard Booth	CLG
John Harrower	CLG
Allan McDougall	CLG
Frank Bowness	CCF
Frank Griffiths	CCF
Norman Hovendon	CCF
Duncan Prior	DoE

Draft prepared by Jim Meikle and Joanna Eley of Davis Langdon Consultancy and funded by the Department of the Environment.

The Construction Industry Board acknowledges the contribution of all of these people with gratitude and the many others who assisted Working Group 3.

Tell us your views

To: The Chief Executive
Construction Industry Board
26 Store Street
London WC1E 7BT

Tel: 0171 636 2256; *Fax:* 0171 637 2258; *Email:* cib@compuserve.com

The CIB is a partnership between the representative bodies of the industry, its clients and government for the improvement of UK construction. We welcome any feedback on the application of this Code of Practice.

Please photocopy this form and use it to send us your views.

Title of report: *Code of practice for the selection of subcontractors,* April 1997

Comments *(please attach any supporting information)*:

Your details:

Name/position/job title . . . .

Company/address . . . .

. . . .

Tel/fax/email . . . .

Date . . . .

Construction Industry *Board*